THIS IS ME! 2022

UK RHYMES

Edited By Reuben Messer

First published in Great Britain in 2022 by:

YoungWriters®
Est. 1991

Young Writers
Remus House
Coltsfoot Drive
Peterborough
PE2 9BF
Telephone: 01733 890066
Website: www.youngwriters.co.uk

All Rights Reserved
Book Design by Ashley Janson
© Copyright Contributors 2022
Softback ISBN 978-1-80015-987-7

Printed and bound in the UK by BookPrintingUK
Website: www.bookprintinguk.com
YB0505K

FOREWORD

For Young Writers' latest competition This Is Me, we asked primary school pupils to look inside themselves, to think about what makes them unique, and then write a poem about it! They rose to the challenge magnificently and the result is this fantastic collection of poems in a variety of poetic styles.

Here at Young Writers our aim is to encourage creativity in children and to inspire a love of the written word, so it's great to get such an amazing response, with some absolutely fantastic poems. It's important for children to focus on and celebrate themselves and this competition allowed them to write freely and honestly, celebrating what makes them great, expressing their hopes and fears, or simply writing about their favourite things. This Is Me gave them the power of words. The result is a collection of inspirational and moving poems that also showcase their creativity and writing ability.

I'd like to congratulate all the young poets in this anthology, I hope this inspires them to continue with their creative writing.

CONTENTS

Al Falah Primary School, Clapton

Salma Nuur (9)	1
Maryam Ali (9)	2
Safiyah Bailey (9)	4
Mohamed Omar (10)	6
Angel Aleesha Ali (9)	8
Sakinah Bailey (9)	10
Ismaeel Kolia (9)	12
Safa Nur (9)	14
Younis Yusuf	15
Sufyan Ahmad (9)	16
Khalid Said (9)	17
Amira Ahmed (9)	18
Safa Sayed (9)	19
Ahmed Jimale (9)	20

Baines Endowed (VC) School, Thornton Cleveleys

Oliver Duerden (11)	21
Finn Bowater & Jacob Wilson	22
Joshua Elson & Bethany Mell (11)	24
Charlotte Sharrock (10) & Sam Graham (10)	26
Layla Ryder & Lilly Forsyth (11)	28
Ethan Hardy (11) & Emma Chieffo	30
Lewis Mcmillan (11) & George Robinson	31
Max Moorhouse (11) & Deacon	32
Poppy Sugden (10) & Oliver	33
Treasure Igiebor & Chloe Gothard	34
Jessica Mcilvennie (10)	35
Tom Smyth (11)	36

Rhys Warwick & Cayden	37
Seth Brownlie Goodrick (10) & George Barrans	38
Isaac Smith (10)	39
Darcey Hart (10)	40

Cardiff Muslim Primary School, Cathays

Hafsa Mehmood (10)	41
Aisha Argin (11)	42
Rahmah Junayed (10)	44
Fizza Aziz (10)	46
Bisma Madni (10)	48
Maryam Alam (11)	49
Anya Ahmed (9)	50
Yacoub Alam (10)	51
Maariyah Rahman (7)	52
Amina Malik (10)	53
Khadijah Ahmed (11)	54
Aaliyah Salah (9)	55
Ibraheem Ahmed (9)	56
Omar Rafi (11)	57
Hassan Aziz (10)	58
Amaani Wallace (8)	59
Iyad Mohammad (7)	60
Aiyoub Miedeck (11)	61
Khalid Ibrahim (8)	62
Safa Rauf (9)	63
Hafsa Argin (8)	64
Aaishah Ahmed (8)	65
Abdullah Chouhdary (8)	66
Omar Mahdi (9)	67
Eesa Hafeez (8)	68
Wesal Hadadi (11)	69
Fathema Islam (8)	70

Name	Number
Eesa Ibrahim (8)	71
Daania Vaqas (8)	72
Safiya Mehmood (9)	73
Rahma Mohamed (10)	74
Aqsa Ahmed (11)	75
Hishaam Sahad (7)	76
Suhayb Hassan (8)	77
Romana Sahad (10)	78
Anas Mohamed (9)	79
Abdullah Wallace (11)	80
Mohamed Awad (9)	81
Zara Al Masud (7)	82
Dawud Hassan (10)	83
Maaz Pitafi (10)	84
Rahma Mohamed (10)	85
Mohammed Ibrahim (10)	86
Maryam Hafeez (9)	87
Yusuf Ibrahim (9)	88
Zikra Sultan (11)	89

Greenbank Preparatory School, Cheadle Hulme

Name	Number
Harris Choudhry (10)	90
Joe Levy (10)	92
Amelia Marsh (11)	93
Charlotte Dicks (10)	94
Seth Hughes (11)	95
Gigi Switzer (10)	96
Yousaf Rafiq (11)	97
Madeleine Lewis (10)	98
George Woolley (10)	99
Neal Vora (10)	100
Ibrahim Ghafoor (10)	101
Zak Martin (10)	102
Dove Nguem (11)	103
Harriet Heinekey (10)	104

Gunter Primary School, Pype Hayes

Name	Number
Poppy Pinkstone (10)	105
Alexandra Edwards (10)	106
Isabell Swinburn (9)	107
Ovander Delaney (9)	108
Micah Robinson (9)	109
Emily Fellows (10)	110
Hermiela Mogos (9)	111
Ayaan Fazil (9)	112
Fidyan Masum (9)	113
Harrison Bird (10)	114
Dewon Montaque (9)	115
Deacon Kelly (10)	116
Marcus Bryant (10)	117
Alfie Conroy (9)	118
Addison Moore (9)	119

Hatfield Woodhouse Primary School, Hatfield Woodhouse

Name	Number
Isaac O'Brien (9)	120
Grayson Golightly (9)	121
Lilly-Mai Ramsey (10)	122
Sophia Wilcock (7)	123
Edward Camplejohn (8)	124
Edward O'Brien (9)	125
Ellis Finney (8)	126
Nancy Wigglesworth (7)	127
Orla Torn (9)	128
Georgia Hornsby (10)	129
Harry Houghton (9)	130
Emma Mikolkova (7)	131
Sophie Kirk (7)	132
Heidi Foster (8)	133
Benjamin Hatton (10)	134
Amelia Dawes (8)	135
Jadon Davies (7)	136
Miriam Daisy Cottingham Taylorson (8)	137
Isabella Watson (10)	138
Oliver Stewart (7)	139
Jacob Jackson (7)	140
Caitlin Beasley (10)	141
Noah Massingham (10)	142
Dale Hibbitt (7)	143
Faye Severn (10)	144
Esme Massingham (8)	145

Langmoor Primary School, Oadby

Orla Caldwell-Giles (7)	146
Lillie Green (7)	148
Charlotte Watts (7)	149
Erin Knight	150
Charlie Picton (7)	151
Tiago Sood (8)	152
Ted Smith (8)	153
Sahib Shergill (8)	154
Fraya Turner (8)	155

Melvich Primary School, Melvich

Kamryn Mackay (9)	156
Merryn Murray (10)	157
Megan Murray (9)	158
Benjamin Mackinnon (10)	159
Stanley Bird (8)	160
Calum Farquhar (10)	161
Emily Farquhar (9)	162
Aurelia Sweeting (8)	163
Mati Ilski (9)	164
Connor Crossley (8)	165

Ryhill Junior, Infant & Nursery School, Ryhill

Jack Hatfield (9)	166
Molly Carr (9)	167
Kate Mclauchlan (9)	168
Freddie Nunn (9)	169
Miller Lee Bramley (9)	170
Scarlett Cadman (8)	171
James Mallinder (9)	172
Callan Church (9)	173
Isla Henderson (8)	174
Tia Earl (10)	175
Max Miller (9)	176
Lilly-May Lawton (8)	177
Evie Broadhead (9)	178
Jesse Bryan (8)	179
Evie Mai Jowitt (9)	180
Freddy Atmore (9)	181

Otis Ferron (8)	182
Joshua Johnson (11)	183
Ben Ellis (9)	184
Lucas Sagar (10)	185
Kade Parkinson (9)	186
Flynn McCabe (8)	187
Lana Cabas (9)	188
Mason Watson (9)	189
Eleanor Hope (10)	190
Amy Corden (10)	191
Lily Alice Wicks (9)	192
Jay Fisher (9)	193
Caiden Armitage (11)	194
Allana Margerrison (10)	195
Eboney Smart (9)	196
Grace Morris (9)	197

Wisbech St Mary CE (VA) Primary School, Wisbech St Mary

Abigail Wielezew (9)	198
Georgie Cordery (10)	200
Riamae Boswell (9)	201
Mercedes Neale	202
Chase Finch (10)	203
Bobby Holmes (9)	204
Sophia Lee (9)	205
Hollie Payne (10)	206
Jazmin New (10)	207
Jack Broker (10)	208
Tillie Bowett (10)	209
Lily Godwin (9)	210
Eve Clark (10)	211
Jake Gilson (9)	212
Ella Jayne Lemmon (9)	213

THE POEMS

Ricado

Day and night,
This gaily bedlight,
Looking for a knight to fight.
Journey's so long,
He sang a song.

From his earliest youth,
Had kept a strict regard from the truth.
And he never knew,
Why life was so true,
Attempted to believe Ricado

This young gloomy knight, gave up a fight,
Growing so old,
He became very bold.
He fell on the ground,
Was never found.

He couldn't move,
But couldn't lose,
In search of the land of Ricado.
His horse had a knife,
Killed him in sight.

Salma Nuur (9)
Al Falah Primary School, Clapton

Fleldorado

As the moon came into the sky,
He found a cave way up high,
As the shadow disappeared and the sunshine came up,
The knight came out and found a cup,
Inside he found a longsword,
He found his energy and went in search for Fleldorado.

He went in the dark cold and miserable,
Looking for the land of Fleldorado,
It was dark and shallow but he kept his promise to find Fleldorado,
He chopped crops,
But there were lots.

In search for Fleldorado,
Searching day and night,
He was about to give up,
Until he found the spirit of Fleldorado,
Follow the bright stars and you will find Fleldorado,
So he went in search for Fleldorado.

He found a map for the land of FIeldorado,
And said, "I will find the land of FIeldorado,"
Just then he found out something,
Something very surprising,
He was already...
On the land of FIeldorado.

Maryam Ali (9)
Al Falah Primary School, Clapton

Cansisco

Beyond the night,
A warrior in fright,
Had journeyed long,
Who was finding the princess Cansisco,
Through the woods of wolves,
Never giving up.

The day was long,
Of the burning heat,
And sandstorms blowing his eyes,
Down the hill,
To climbing the highest mountains,
Striving to his quest.

Days go by,
He lay in the grass,
Looking up to the sky,
Saying, "Where should I possibly go?"
He shuffles through the flowers,
Climbs trees and walks back.

Years go by,
A waste of time,

Finding a lost princess,
Out of the blue,
This didn't sound true,
He found a gloomy girl,
Dance and prance,
By the river,
He gazed at her running,
Taking her back,
To the castle.

Safiyah Bailey (9)
Al Falah Primary School, Clapton

The Land Of Belfua

The brave knight,
Who was searching for something that turned day to night,
The land of Belfua,
A genie was just waiting there,
In the land of Belfua.

This knight so bold,
He turned very old,
He looked for the land,
And heard something that sounded like a band,
The land of Belfua.

The land of Belfua,
So very cold,
The knight finally found it,
The land of Belfua,
Jumping up and down.

The genie was surprised,
An old knight like him,
Found a genie like him,

In the land of Belfua,
A place so secret.

The genie interrogated him,
But the knight was not afraid of him,
The genie started to trust the knight,
But the knight thought he wanted to fight.

Mohamed Omar (10)
Al Falah Primary School, Clapton

Zenphine

A dedicated knight,
Nobody else in sight,
Always looking for a fight,
From day to night,
In search of Zenphine.

I travelled so long,
I made up a song,
But still always feeling down,
Never stop thinking of Zenphine.

And at his youth,
Sadly he knew the truth,
He met a shadow,
"Zenphine," he stated,
This woman called Zenphine.

Over the waterfall,
Just wait and listen for the call,
Follow the sound,
If you seek for Zenphine.

I am finally here,
But there is nobody near,
The shadow has lied,
I shouldn't have followed his guide,
I will find you Zenphine.

Angel Aleesha Ali (9)
Al Falah Primary School, Clapton

Ragadado

In the gloomy night,
With no one in sight,
Had journeyed long,
In search of the shadow,
In search of Ragadado.

He travelled so long,
Each day comes,
He gets very old,
Fell, as he found,
Something on the ground,
That looked like someone was around though,
In search of Ragadado.

And as his strength,
Failed him at length,
And he found a meadow,
"What is that?" said he,
"Where can it be?"
"The land of Ragadado," said he.

Down the meadow,
Over the trees,

A bumpy ride,
If you seek for Ragadado.

Sakinah Bailey (9)
Al Falah Primary School, Clapton

The Old Brave Knight

On a dark night,
There was a knight,
Not a normal one,
But a good one,
Searching for treasure.

But he grew old,
Over sixty years old,
He was weak,
But could not help it,
He still was searching,
And never would give up.

He grew older and older,
Now he was weaker,
He was still not giving up,
Even if everyone said,
He was still looking for treasure,
The best one ever.

He was walking,
But he fell down,
He fainted,

People tried to wake him,
But he did not wake,
Then they found out he died.

Ismaeel Kolia (9)
Al Falah Primary School, Clapton

Eldoraldo

And as her strength,
Failed her at length,
She met a loud lion,
"Lion," she said,
"Where can it be,
This land of Eldoraldo?"

"Over the houses,
Over the clouds,
By the moon,
Near the secret door,"
The loud lion replied,
"If you see for that land."

Then she said,
"Thank you so much,
Because you saved my life."
The lion replied,
"You're welcome but I have to hide."

Safa Nur (9)
Al Falah Primary School, Clapton

The Great Treasure

A pirate so unwise,
He just wanted to rise,
But he fell down,
And the only thing on his face was a frown.

But he set sail,
Not just to be pale,
He got defeated,
But not deleted.

He fought a dragon,
Shot a cannon,
But he killed a doughnut-eating man,
And mistakenly kicked a can.

But still in search of the great treasure,
Still killed a beast,
In search of the great treasure,
For the sake of his pleasure.

Younis Yusuf
Al Falah Primary School, Clapton

Until He Finds Maximarco

Decorated nicely,
A brave young knight,
On his quest,
Looking for Maximarco.

It's been sixty years,
He's gone all weak,
He can't walk on his feet,
Still looking for Maximarco.

Down the mountain,
His horse had died,
Ten years later,
Now walking to the grave of Maximarco.

Walking with his shield,
Found a tiger,
"Go over there," he said,
That's the grave of Maximarco.

Sufyan Ahmad (9)
Al Falah Primary School, Clapton

Eldorado

He searched day and night,
Over the mountains,
Over the moon,
Then he found the mysterious land of Eldorado.

He found a palace,
And suddenly saw Eldorado,
He got a knife,
And ended his life.

He found some treasure,
And ended with pleasure,
His treasure was a princess,
But she was in a mess.

The knight hurried,
And then they got married,
Then he felt sorry,
And the forest became foggy.

Khalid Said (9)
Al Falah Primary School, Clapton

Alborano

Modestly dressed,
A consistent knight,
Won't give up a fight,
In search for Alborano.

But he grew old,
This sensible man,
But soon there was a shadow,
That looked like Alborano.

This shadow he asked,
I must find this land,
She is my queen,
This land called Alborano.

Under the mountain of the dragon,
Through the swamp,
Ride the bumpy ride,
In search for Alborano.

Amira Ahmed (9)
Al Falah Primary School, Clapton

The Brave Knight

When the moon came into the sky,
The knight found a cave a little high,
The knight went to sleep,
He thought about the cave he should keep.

When the sun came up,
He found a cup,
The knight went to the waterfall,
He almost fell with a bird's call.

Years went by,
Just a waste of time,
He grew so old,
About fifty years old,
But he never gave up.

Safa Sayed (9)
Al Falah Primary School, Clapton

One Piece

A bold pirate,
With shining treasure,
Searching the seas,
For the one piece.

One day, his ship wrecked,
All he said was, "All on deck!"
He had to build his ship,
In order to find the one piece.

They eventually set sail,
Everybody was so pale,
They finally found the one piece.

Ahmed Jimale (9)
Al Falah Primary School, Clapton

The Day Bravery Came To Visit

The clouds shone with bravery and the sun proudly pushed its confident self out to be seen,
It was because of the brave soul strolling along the street,
The pavement progressing boldness beneath his feet,
He knocked on my wooded door with another huge brave grin.

I answered the door and a powerful courageous gust of wind flew at me,
His eyes stood his ground,
And a jet-black coat hooded his gallant calculations,
We went to the park and travelled far,
We just went everywhere in his confident car.

But of course friendship will come to an end but bravery will never end,
I watched him go and create someone else's life,
But to be honest, we will always be friends.

Oliver Duerden (11)
Baines Endowed (VC) School, Thornton Cleveleys

The Day Silliness Came To Visit

Silliness walked down the street,
Humming himself a goofy beat,
He stumbled into my dining room,
He broke down the door, it fell with a boom.

He had a bright pink shirt that glistened like the moon,
On his purple hair lay an out of place hat,
It was bright green and looked oddly flat,
He did a little dance and picked up my cat.

Suddenly, he broke into song,
"Your cat is a cat, really cute and fat."
"My name is silliness, I'll teach you all about that."
I dropped my food, it fell to the floor with a splat.

I looked into his wild, goofy green eyes,
As I did so I got a surprise,
Silliness had gathered all the pots and pans,
And was juggling them, (with his bare hands!)

As he was doing this, I felt a chuckle rise in my throat,
He picked up an avocado and made it float,
I felt an urge to join him as he made a sugar paper boat,
It was amazing! (But I'm not trying to gloat.)

He plucked some food out of thin air,
There were chocolate bars and chocolate cakes everywhere!
My heart sank as he went to the door,
But suddenly, he pulled something out of his pocket.

It was red, gold and bright,
And looked like a firework rocket,
He waved to me and with a bang and a flair,
He was gone into the midnight air.

Finn Bowater & Jacob Wilson
Baines Endowed (VC) School, Thornton Cleveleys

The Day That Joy Came To Visit

Joy gracefully strolled down the street,
Happily greeting people they meet,
Dancing and swirling at the door,
They gently tap with a *knock-knock*.

With their eyes filled with happiness,
They waited patiently to greet me,
Joy wore beautiful dresses that were filled with vibrant colours of the radiant rainbow.

When I saw them, I felt immediate delightfulness,
We sang merry songs all day long,
Which we did until Big Ben chimed *ding-dong*.

We ate scrumptious biscuits and delicious fairy cakes,
Whilst we drank cups of tea sticking out our pinkies.

Holding hands tightly, we floated back to their beloved home and whispered farewell,
Ready to carry the journey on to tomorrow.
The next time joy comes around, we'll go to the park and have a splendid picnic.

Joy is something you feel inside,
Joy is something that you cannot hide.

Joshua Elson & Bethany Mell (11)
Baines Endowed (VC) School, Thornton Cleveleys

The Day That Silliness Came To Visit

The sound of a plane,
Then a smash of some glass!
And a laugh as loud as thunder,
As he clumsily roles through the smashed open window.
I peeked through the door,
Only to see,
A half-broken window,
And a hyper-looking figure staring at me.
His eyes were so bright,
What a wonderful sight,
He wore a clown-looking outfit,
That went down to his knees,
And a pie in his hand,
That was pointing at me!
I looked at Silliness,
Then I decided to run.
Being blinded by the sun,
When I saw him chasing me,
I felt like I was about to pee!

We ran up the road,
And back down again,
Then decided to meet,
In the middle of the street.
Then we came in and ate,
Some chocolate cake,
Until we were full and it was getting late.
He jumped back out the window,
Into his plane,
Never to be seen that day again.

Charlotte Sharrock (10) & Sam Graham (10)
Baines Endowed (VC) School, Thornton Cleveleys

The Day That Love Came To Visit

He came walking along the hard stone path,
He would knock on the door as light as a feather.
His eyes were sapphire-blue and they were glistening like the seawater,
He would wear a plain T-shirt, grey ripped jeans and a leather black jacket,
He had a beautiful Labrador that would always come with him.
When I saw him I had butterflies in my stomach,
At the same time I was excited to see him.
We went to the grassy park with a wonderful lake and had a lovely picnic while we watched the sunset.
Soon after we had dinner and we really enjoyed it.
He is a very messy eater but he still made me laugh.
He left with a cute smile and a cuddle and said goodbye.
After that I knew he was the one for me,

I felt that way ever since.
He always took good care of me and he was the kindest person I ever met.

Layla Ryder & Lilly Forsyth (11)
Baines Endowed (VC) School, Thornton Cleveleys

The Day That Silliness Came To Visit

Silliness unicycled down the street and arrived at my house,
He honked the air horn and woke me up.
When I opened the door I saw that he had really whopping glasses on with rainbow pipe cleaners on them.
He wore a clown suit with crazy, colourful hair, his face was painted with many colours.
Dragging his things into the house, he left a trail of glitter on the doorstep.
He entertained me by riding his unicycle and juggled around me.
We ate tacos and drank a large bottle of Coke, he made me laugh by drinking like a dog.
We saluted to each other and he rode away.
The next time he comes round, we will try to do the Coke and Mentos experiment.
He reminds me of the circus.

Ethan Hardy (11) & Emma Chieffo
Baines Endowed (VC) School, Thornton Cleveleys

The Day That Kindness Came To Visit

Skipping joyfully down the street,
Kindness arrived at my door,
When I saw him I felt fulfilled,
He played some music and performed a dance,
He was the nicest person you will ever meet.

His eyes shone like diamonds in the sun,
Then he asked me if I want to have some fun,
He wore a pastel blue shirt,
We started to dance and sing some songs,
But then my feet started to hurt.

We went to the theme park,
We shared a large fluffy candyfloss.

We said our goodbyes and tears filled my eyes,
The next time kindness comes around,
We'll go to the park and play on the swings,
They remind me of my precious family.

Lewis Mcmillan (11) & George Robinson
Baines Endowed (VC) School, Thornton Cleveleys

The Day Silliness Came To Visit

Silliness ran down the street,
Pretending to ride a striped balloon,
Ringing my doorbell a million times,
His large eyes were purple,
And he wore a rainbow suit with a rainbow cane.

When I saw him I felt silly,
And felt full of joy.
We cartwheeled down the lane,
Pounding drums and prank-called,
Every fast food place we could find.

We drank so many fizzy drinks,
And saw who could burp the loudest,
We ate so many sweets,
We began to feel sick and almost threw up.

Then he pretended his cane was a horse,
And off he rode down the street,
To cause mischief somewhere else.

Max Moorhouse (11) & Deacon
Baines Endowed (VC) School, Thornton Cleveleys

The Day Silliness Came To Visit

Silliness came on a clown unicycle,
Laughing and joking around,
He came without warning,
And went *rat-a-tat* on my door.
He wore large rainbow overalls covered in paint,
He came with a smile on his rosy-red face,
His eyes were emerald-green and shimmered in the sun,
And his hair was the colour of a day full of fun.
We went to the park,
And ate ice cream,
Played football with our friends.
We drank bubble tea,
Ate cotton candy,
And we drank drinks by the beach,
Until...
Suddenly it was time to go!
I gave him a hug,
And we said goodbye,
As a tear dropped out of my eye.

Poppy Sugden (10) & Oliver
Baines Endowed (VC) School, Thornton Cleveleys

The Day That Silliness Came To Town

Silliness, crazily drove up the street in his colourful clown mobile,
He hopped out and threw water balloons at the window.
I opened the door and his long springy ginger hair bounced in my face,
His big shiny smile hypnotised me.
With him was my biggest fear... A fake spider!
When I saw him I felt happy but annoyed.
We prank-called Starbucks and asked for a burger,
We laughed our heads off until they actually came off.
We ate sweets that made our feet stink.
He said goodbye by trumping in my face,
And his fart spelled out the letters 'Goodbye'
The next time Silliness comes around I'll prank him back.

Treasure Igiebor & Chloe Gothard
Baines Endowed (VC) School, Thornton Cleveleys

The Day Kindness Walked In

As Kindness skipped beautifully down the street whistling a merry tune,
They knocked gently on the wooden door,
Their appearance was gorgeous they had baby blue eyes and a pastel hoodie,
And had an adorable ferret with them,
When I saw them I felt my eyes bulging, because of their beauty.
We went out to walk along the beach and got ice cream and doughnuts and drank hot chocolate.
They ploughed through the waves,
And at the end of it all we got a coffee and said goodbye with a much needed hug.
Hopefully next time she will bring her friends over.

Jessica Mcilvennie (10)
Baines Endowed (VC) School, Thornton Cleveleys

The Day Kindness Came To Visit

Kindness skipped down my street,
And knocked on my door very lightly.

I answered and saw a bright woman,
She wore a colourful dress,
And her blue eyes sparkled in the sunlight,
When I saw her I felt full with joy.

We went for a hot brew,
And started to feel blue,
We ate some noodles.

But of course she had to make someone else's life better,
We hugged and said goodbye.

Tom Smyth (11)
Baines Endowed (VC) School, Thornton Cleveleys

The Day Bravery Came To Visit

The day bravery saved the world,
His iron fist pounded at the magnificent steel door.
A shiny sword scraped across the brick walls,
She wore a gown made of angel hair,
When I saw her I felt a bond,
A flower just about to bloom,
We asked each other about life,
My friend gave me a hug and wished me a good day,
Then reminded me to care for my family.

Rhys Warwick & Cayden
Baines Endowed (VC) School, Thornton Cleveleys

The Day That Anger Came To Town

They arrived on a raging bull,
Stamping around the living room, lobbing the TV and flipping the chairs,
Their eyes were bloodshot like a roaring devil,
They had bulging muscles like giant boulders and his face was ruby-red,
When I saw them I felt petrified,
We broke people's houses and threw twigs at people,
We ate some raw fish and live chickens.

Seth Brownlie Goodrick (10) & George Barrans
Baines Endowed (VC) School, Thornton Cleveleys

The Day Silliness Came To Visit

He stumbled across the street,
Pounded his head on the door and fell over.
He wore a clown costume and had a bucket of water.
When I saw him I felt confused and suspicious.
We ate a cow pie and a pig's nose.
Then we said goodbye
And ate some pie.
The next time he comes around we'll go skydiving.

Isaac Smith (10)
Baines Endowed (VC) School, Thornton Cleveleys

The Day That Joy Came To Visit

Joy who is a boy,
Happily skipped down the street,
And rang the doorbell.
With his eyes sparkling in the sun,
With his pretty red balloon.
When I saw him I felt happy that he had just filled the room with joy.
We sat down and had a cup of tea,
And said bye.

Darcey Hart (10)
Baines Endowed (VC) School, Thornton Cleveleys

All About Me!

In school they call me a rocket,
I always have something in my pocket,
I do maths problems until I've got it,
Around my neck I like to wear a locket,
I am amazing at baking,
But not too patient at waiting,
I love doing painting,
And enjoy creating,
I enjoy organising by colour,
My friends say I'm a good runner,
I like to do things my way,
But that doesn't always happen in the day!
I do swimming, basketball and drama,
When I grow up I want to get a llama!
Sometimes I tell my dad to be calmer,
And he says he should have been a farmer.

My name is Hafsa,
I go with the flow,
Watch me grow.

Hafsa Mehmood (10)
Cardiff Muslim Primary School, Cathays

This Is Me!

I'm honest, I'm kind, I've got a smart and quick mind,
I left Cardiff and started a new life,
I moved to Kuwait and I couldn't wait,
I spent eight years there and now I'm back at the square,
I love doing art I just don't know where to start,
My family is my life, I might want to be a midwife,
Maths is my superpower, I could do it in the shower,
I am bright and full of might, you wouldn't want to start a fight,
I am creative, I could be persuasive and I am surely initiative,
Cats give me a fright because I'm scared they might fight,
Sometimes I may flower depending on the hour,
My mum says I'm thoughtful, the complete opposite of faultful.
I pray five times a day, it is only fair I give back to Allah who made me aware,
It's the only way I can repair as well as prepare,

So this is me,
Hopefully soon getting a degree!

Aisha Argin (11)
Cardiff Muslim Primary School, Cathays

All About Me

My name is Rahmah,
I'm in Year 5,
Let me explain about my life.
Appearance-wise, I am average size,
I have brown eyes and long black hair,
My skin isn't exactly fair.

I have many talents that flow within me,
Like the mesmerising harmony of the stretched out sea,
I'm obsessed with books, I'm learning how to cook,
I'm good with art, well at least that's a start.
I go to cubs, no other clubs,
They make me feel so good inside,
I'm free to laugh, make jokes and proudly stride.

I've travelled all around the world,
Like a dove elegantly flying.
From the spectacle above the land was a big swirl,
Definitely no denying.

My background is Bengali,
Pakistani too,

The thing that completes our culture,
Is the most delicious scrumptious food.

Rahmah Junayed (10)
Cardiff Muslim Primary School, Cathays

Fantastic Amazing Me

My name is Fizza,
I hate pizza,
My favourite colour is yellow,
I get a little mellow,
My role model is my mum,
With her I have fun,
She is like the sun,
I am loyal,
But not royal,
My dad keeps us in line,
Everything else is fine,
Most of the time,
I don't play football,
But I go to the mall,
I have a lovely school,
Which is nice and cool,
I have a great life,
I don't want to be a midwife,
I have a lovely family,
Which is Pakistani,
And that isn't the end of me,

Be happy,
This is me!

Fizza Aziz (10)
Cardiff Muslim Primary School, Cathays

All About Me

When I see the ocean and shells my heart turns navy blue,
When I see the galaxy my heart feels dreamy,
I could stare at it all night.
When I see a red rose my heart turns into a real rose.
When I see the hot blood orange sun I feel like a star.
My favourite colour galaxy makes me an artistic girl.
When I'm older I want to be a fashion designer and an artist and a swimming teacher and a photographer and an author and also so many other things.
When I hear the Quran my heart feels soft,
And when I pray my heart goes into another world.

Bisma Madni (10)
Cardiff Muslim Primary School, Cathays

Marvellous Majestic Maryam

Tall, dark and curly,
That's who I am... surely.
But I am so much more than my appearance,
I'm kind and smart,
And I love my parents.
Eldest of four siblings,
I really am a pro,
I truly love my family,
Of that, I really know.
Swimming and kickboxing are my game,
Or perhaps baking is where I find my fame.
A midwife I would like to be,
Or optician to help people see,
So you see I'm so much more than my appearance,
That's what comes with having perseverance.

Maryam Alam (11)
Cardiff Muslim Primary School, Cathays

All About Me, A Sense Poem About Me

My name is Anya,
I am nine,
When I look at the sun I feel bright and light.
When I look at the galaxy,
I feel very sparkly.
When I listen to the Quran,
I feel very calm.
At a blink of an eye,
I am wise.
I've wanted to be everything!
I look at the sea,
My heart turns very blue,
I always look for clues.
I want to be a spy and I want to be a doctor.
When I look at the moon,
I feel very shiny white.
I am enthusiastic,
I love being me don't you see?

Anya Ahmed (9)
Cardiff Muslim Primary School, Cathays

Things That Spark About Me!

I may be skinny my face is always grinny,
I look at my friends' faces their faces shine bright,
But mine is as sharp as light,
Just look up in the stars you'll see my smile,
My smile is as blue as the Nile.

I may be ten, at least I'm older than a hen.
People make fun of my name but they will gossip in shame.

Swimming is where I find my fame,
But football is where I find my name.

Thank you for listening to my rhyme,
I hope I didn't waste your time.

Yacoub Alam (10)
Cardiff Muslim Primary School, Cathays

All About Me

A bag full of love from Manchester
Sparkling water from the lush rivers of Cardiff
Bakes a sweet lemon in 2014
This is me!

A pinch of sugar and a pinch of salt
Some say I'm sweet and others call me sour!
But it really doesn't matter, this is me forever
She's 100% bananas and 50% chocolate
Add a drop of milk and you get a flower
Who is 110cm tall just like a tower!

This is me who buzzes like a bee
Likes to eat honey
This is all about me!

Maariyah Rahman (7)
Cardiff Muslim Primary School, Cathays

My Colour Poem

C is for how I love cute and crazy cats,
O is for how I love tangy, sweet oranges,
L is for how I like sour lemons,
O is for how I love athletic orangutans,
U is for how I adore yummy Uber Eats,
R is for how I love really fluffy rabbits.

P is for how I adore my parents,
O is for how I hate the colour orange,
E is for how I extremely love Eid,
M is for how I love marvellous movies.

Amina Malik (10)
Cardiff Muslim Primary School, Cathays

This Is Me!

My parents named me Khadijah,
After the mother of history's greatest nation,
The first to believe, the first to have faith,
As Khadijah was a role model in history,
Who led Muslims to victory,
I aspire to be just like her,
To be kind and loving to all,
I am knowledgeable, helpful, amazing, delightful,
Inspiring, just, awesome and honest, just like her.

I like my name, it's special to me,
It's exactly who I want to be!

Khadijah Ahmed (11)
Cardiff Muslim Primary School, Cathays

All About Me

A m I someone you know? Well, no
A little room for me and a big one for my younger brothers but I don't really mind because it's pretty
L ove everyone around me so I care for everyone
I think I know a bit of maths but it is still okay
Y ay, I'm always happy and everyone should be
A is in my brother's, my mum and my name
H ow happy can I be? Well, do you know me now?

Aaliyah Salah (9)
Cardiff Muslim Primary School, Cathays

The Colours Of My Life

When I see animals my loving heart is deep red,
Just like a rose.

When I hear the waves in the ocean my heart immediately feels a stroke of blue,
Just like the waves.

When I smell candles my heart instantly feels a magenta-like pink.

When I feel the touch of a very soft cushion,
The colour orange comes straight to my mind.

When I taste rice,
The colour gold instantly comes to my heart.

Ibraheem Ahmed (9)
Cardiff Muslim Primary School, Cathays

Omar The Cricketer

My name is Omar,
I have black hair,
I have a nose that has a hole,
I like playing cricket,
I always get a wicket,
My celebration is always a racket,
You will never see me with a jacket,
Even in winter,
I don't shiver,
I like eating a burger,
As it takes away my hunger,
And makes me larger,
One day I'll be a cricketer,
One day I'll be a winner and give everyone chicken dinner!

Omar Rafi (11)
Cardiff Muslim Primary School, Cathays

All About Me

My name is Hassan,
I like playing football,
I love my family.
Happy to mention of course,
Some people are Pakistani,
Well so am I,
Me and my brother love to spy!
To earn my respect you need kindness,
Everyone needs this!
I am Muslim,
I am glad,
Whoever isn't shouldn't be mad.
Some say I am a fun-killer,
And some say I'm a good footballer.
This is me!
Hassan Aziz, peace!

Hassan Aziz (10)
Cardiff Muslim Primary School, Cathays

All About Me!

- **A** mazing at writing
- **M** agnificent mind
- **A** stonishing at spelling
- **A** mazing and funny
- **N** ice and helpful
- **I** ncredible person

- **W** onderful knowledge
- **A** uthentic in all situations
- **L** uckily going to a good school
- **L** ovely and kind
- **A** wesome and cool
- **C** alm and active
- **E** nthusiastic and I have a big heart.

Amaani Wallace (8)
Cardiff Muslim Primary School, Cathays

This Is Me! Bake Me!

Take a bucketful of football,
A tablespoon of family and friends,
Scoop three kilograms of confidence,
This is me! Football me!

Add a jugful of generosity,
Sprinkle three litres of speed and strength,
A tablespoon of happiness,
This is me! Epic me!

Sprinkle a spoonful of faith,
Whisk a spoon of love,
Pour a jugful of kindness,
Make me or break me, this is me!

Iyad Mohammad (7)
Cardiff Muslim Primary School, Cathays

This Is Me

My name is Aiyoub,
I came from a land far far away,
You might have seen me but not know me!

My dream is to go back to where I belong,
I pray and hope my waiting won't be long.

I love basketball as it's exciting and fun,
I want to achieve and be the one!

The great player that shows the world who I really am,
So watch me fill the crowd, my beloved future fan!

Aiyoub Miedeck (11)
Cardiff Muslim Primary School, Cathays

This Is Me Recipe!

Stir in some family and friends,
Spread some giggles and more,
Scoop some speed and devotion,
This is me! Rare me!

Take a spoonful of love,
Whisk kilograms of reading,
Add bucketsful of faith,
This is me! Football theme!

Add a glass of footballs,
Mix laughter and memories,
Pour a bowl of happiness and hugs,
Mix me or leave me!
This is me! Amazing me!

Khalid Ibrahim (8)
Cardiff Muslim Primary School, Cathays

What Am I Like?

My name is Safa and I'm nine years old,
I'm very sporty, but not such a shorty,
I also like to eat roti but thankfully I'm not such a fatty,
My favourite place to go is the shopping centre because I never take no for an answer,
I like to annoy my brother and try to be kind to every other,
I try my best with everything I do,
I try even harder if I'm with...

You!

Safa Rauf (9)
Cardiff Muslim Primary School, Cathays

This Is Me! Taste Me!

Whisk in five tablespoons of devotion,
Add in ten kilograms of knowledge,
Spread a scoop of special family and friends,
This is me!

Pour in a bucketful of basketball,
Mix in some memories,
Spread in ten kilograms of swimming,
This is me! Taste me!

Sprinkle in a pocketful of speed,
Spread in ten grams of giggles,
Add a bucketful of faith,
This is me! Race me!

Hafsa Argin (8)
Cardiff Muslim Primary School, Cathays

Lovely Me

A aishah loves school,
A nd has two best friends,
I love my family,
S o kind and nice,
H appy me,
A lways have a smile on my face,
H elping all the time.

A aishah is the best!
H as the best work,
M y family is important to me,
E ating all the time,
D id you like my acrostic poem?

Aaishah Ahmed (8)
Cardiff Muslim Primary School, Cathays

This Is Me Recipe!

A bucket of coolness,
Take ten kilograms of knowledge,
Sprinkle in lots of joy,
This is me! Amazing super me!

Mix in a teaspoon of hugs,
Mix in a bowl of devotion,
Sprinkle in some giggles,
This is me! Haha! Amazing!

Get one bowl of friends, amazing friends,
Mix ten bowls of love,
Make ten grams of family,
Bake it or make it, this is super me!

Abdullah Chouhdary (8)
Cardiff Muslim Primary School, Cathays

This Is Me!

This is me!
My name is Omar Mahdi,
I've got short black hair,
With a smile that's never bare,
I want to be an engineer,
And make cars full of cheer,
Like an Aston or a Kia,
And drive them super fast,
And I hope they last,
My background is Iraq,
I eat curry that is sweet,
And a temperature that's neat,
So that is my poem,
All about me.

Omar Mahdi (9)
Cardiff Muslim Primary School, Cathays

This Is Me Recipe

Whisk in a jug of joy,
Pour in ninety kilograms of knowledge,
Take a scoop of super speed,
This is me! Epic glee.

Get a box of memories,
Bring in ninety-nine tubs of reading,
Sprinkle lots of family and friends,
This is me! He hehe.

Open a kilogram of love,
Sprinkle some Salah,
Mix in lots of prayers to Allah,
Make it or take it, this is me.

Eesa Hafeez (8)
Cardiff Muslim Primary School, Cathays

This Is Me!

My name is Wesal,
I live in Cardiff, Wales,
I am a normal girl,
I was born in Saudi, lived there two years,
It's my second year in Cardiff,
Lived in America for five years and a half,
I like basketball and not a lot of football,
I would like to be an investigator or a doctor,
I am a smart, helpful, sometimes creative,
I am quiet but confident.

Wesal Hadadi (11)
Cardiff Muslim Primary School, Cathays

This Is Me Recipe!

Take a spoon of memories,
Pour in a jug of family,
Mix in a little bit of swimming,
This is me!

Sprinkle two spoons of faith,
Add a bottle of knowledge,
Drop in some friends,
This is me, amazing me!

Scoop in a bucket of kindness,
Add in lots of love,
Sprinkle in some jiggly joy,
Love it or leave it, this is me!

Fathema Islam (8)
Cardiff Muslim Primary School, Cathays

This Is Me!

A bucket of speed,
Take a tablespoon of memories,
Whisk in a kilogram of knowledge,
This is me.

Pour in a bucket of faith,
Mix in money,
Whisk in a tablespoon of laughter,
This is me.

Add in a jug of joy,
Sprinkle in some kindness,
Pour in some generosity,
This is me take it or leave it this is me.

Eesa Ibrahim (8)
Cardiff Muslim Primary School, Cathays

This Is Me Recipe!

Take a spoonful of joy,
Pour a cup of love,
Add a tablespoonful of happiness,
This is me! Epic! Me!

Take one cup of hugs,
Pour a jug of family,
Add a cup of knowledge,
This is me! Hehehe!

Pour a bucket of faith,
Take a spoonful of laughter,
Take a cup of reading,
Take it or leave it, this is me!

Daania Vaqas (8)
Cardiff Muslim Primary School, Cathays

I Am Safiya!

I am nice,
I am from those whom call me kind,
But I'm not good at waiting,
Especially when I'm making or shaking,
A bottle of vanilla icing.
I love to change my clothes many times a day,
I like to do it my own way.
It doesn't matter what other people say,
This is me and I always have a fantastic idea to say.

Safiya Mehmood (9)
Cardiff Muslim Primary School, Cathays

Radical Righteous Rahma

This is my rhyme,
It's not yours it's mine.
Basketball's the game,
It stimulates the brain.
Banoffee too smooth,
I want to do a move.
Move too cool,
I want to go to school.
Dua in the day,
I want to pray.
Friends so radical,
I want to be magical.
Love my fam,
We don't eat ham.

Rahma Mohamed (10)
Cardiff Muslim Primary School, Cathays

Learn About Me!

I'm a girl with no curls,
I like to write and see light,
I have glasses but also ashes,
I am eleven with a passion,
I am cheerful but also helpful,
You'll love my imagination and determination,
I like summer with no bummers,
I love tech with a check,
I love games with a change.
This is me!

Aqsa Ahmed (11)
Cardiff Muslim Primary School, Cathays

This Is Me Recipe!

Mix in some happiness,
Add some reading,
Scoop in some knowledge,
This is me!

Scoop in some swimming,
Add a bucketful of boxing,
Pour in some speed,
This is me hehe!

Stir some giggles,
Mix in your friends, whichever one you like!
Sprinkle some joy,
This is me hahaha!

Hishaam Sahad (7)
Cardiff Muslim Primary School, Cathays

All About Me!

S uccessful in school
U nbelievably kind
H elpful all the time
A mazing at sports
Y oung and tall
B right boy

H appy every day
A wesome friend
S harp boy
S weet smile
A lways laughing
N ice and honest.

Suhayb Hassan (8)
Cardiff Muslim Primary School, Cathays

Recipe Poem

Strawberry is sweet, makes my attitude so sweet
Lime is so sour, makes my attitude so sour
Pepper is so spicy, makes my attitude so spicy
Ice cream is so cold, makes my attitude have a brain freeze
Chocolate is so sugary, makes my attitude have a sugar rush
If you want to know about me, then read my recipe!

Romana Sahad (10)
Cardiff Muslim Primary School, Cathays

Acrostic Poem

A mazing
N ice
A wesome,
S ea is cool like me

M ountains are my style
O utside on the beach
H ours and hours making sandcastles
A wesome at maths
M ad about football
E gypt is my home
D ashing in the desert.

Anas Mohamed (9)
Cardiff Muslim Primary School, Cathays

This Is Me!

This is me, this is me,
You can't change me, I'm exactly who I want to be,
Before my life was like a mysterious door without a key,
A colourful bird waiting on a tree,
At my age, I'm like a new seed,
Under the ground, I can't be seen,
I don't fit in because this is me.

Abdullah Wallace (11)
Cardiff Muslim Primary School, Cathays

This Is Me

M arvellous writing,
O ptimistic mind,
H ealthy lifestyle,
A mazing football,
M aximum maths,
E nthusiastic at all times,
D octor I am.

A bsolutely genuine,
W owee,
A mazing,
D rawing is my life.

Mohamed Awad (9)
Cardiff Muslim Primary School, Cathays

This Is Me

Seven tablespoons of happiness,
A cup of love,
A packet of joy,
This is me!

Add a bowl of kindness,
Sprinkle some laughter,
Put in ten grams of painting,
This is me!

Get a handful of friends,
Pour in some family,
Put in a tablespoon of hugs,
This is me!

Zara Al Masud (7)
Cardiff Muslim Primary School, Cathays

All About Me

My name's Dawud,
I know my maths,
Though a lot might know it's not what I like.
When the rugby's on I go crazy,
That might explain why nobody,
Wants to sit next to me!
I've got a big head to fit in the maths,
I've got no more space so it's about to explode!

Dawud Hassan (10)
Cardiff Muslim Primary School, Cathays

The Whale In The Sea

I always see a whale in the sea,
Looking for someone to meet,
It's swimming in pure heat,
Jumping happily like a frog,
Swimming faster than a wave,
The whale, the whale is very brave,
I pet the whale, gently every day,
One day, I will be friends with it and swim.

Maaz Pitafi (10)
Cardiff Muslim Primary School, Cathays

All About Me Rahma Mohamed

My name is Rahma,
I am very smart,
I have a big red kind loving heart.
I'd like to stop a fight,
And bring some light,
Into this world.
I don't like to lie,
But I would say hi and bye.
I love to do art,
But let's have a final caring part.

Rahma Mohamed (10)
Cardiff Muslim Primary School, Cathays

This Is Me!

My name is Mo,
I'm in Year 5,
I have a brother,
He's in Year 3.

I like swimming, Minecraft,
And some loyalty.

Whenever I have problems,
It always nags me.

Hope I see you next time,
Because I know how to share the rhyme!

Mohammed Ibrahim (10)
Cardiff Muslim Primary School, Cathays

About Me Maryam

M aryam's the name,
A nd my big smile's my fame,
R ely on me to stop the shame,
Y ou can gossip in pride,
A nd I won't hide,
M y poem has come to an end.

Maryam Hafeez (9)
Cardiff Muslim Primary School, Cathays

This Is Me

T rue gamer,
H eroic,
I deal,
S ensational footballer.

I nventive and little
S mall.

M agnificent boy,
E xceptional eater.

Yusuf Ibrahim (9)
Cardiff Muslim Primary School, Cathays

This Is Me!

Z ooming fast like a cheetah,
I ntelligent like Einstein,
K ind-hearted like a rose,
R espectful to all humans,
A wesome just like the sun.

Zikra Sultan (11)
Cardiff Muslim Primary School, Cathays

These Are The Ingredients That Make Me

What you need:
A tablespoon of kindness,
A teaspoon of messiness,
A pinch of curiosity,
A dash of fun,
One small mixing bowl,
A whisk,
A cake tin.

How to make it:
First, put your tablespoons of kindness into your small mixing bowl
Preheat your oven to one hundred and eighty degrees.
Second, sprinkle your pinch of curiosity into the mixing bowl
Then throw on a dash of fun and a teaspoon of messiness
Then start to whisk it for ten to fifteen minutes.
Third, put it into your cake tin then in the oven for thirty minutes.

Then let it cool for twenty minutes
Those are the ingredients to make the loving, fun, spectacular me.

Harris Choudhry (10)
Greenbank Preparatory School, Cheadle Hulme

Me

To make a Joe,
Here's what you need to know!

First, a mop of bouncy blonde hair,
Second, add bright brown eyes and a friendly smile,
Then throw in ears for listening and teeth to chomp,
And make me fairly tall with strong legs to stomp.

Now the important final bits we need to chuck in,
Tonnes of laughs,
Soft purring kittens,
Star Wars movies and Lego all day,
And brothers with whom I can play.

Stir well and leave to rest for half a day,
Then tip me out onto a bundle of hay.

You will see I am loyal, kind and caring,
This recipe is one you should be sharing.

Joe Levy (10)
Greenbank Preparatory School, Cheadle Hulme

This Is Me

One cup of funny with a dash of happy,
One cup of loveable with a sprinkle of caring,
One cup of worry with a drop of sensitive,
One cup of family with a scatter of friends,
One teaspoon of shyness,
Two tablespoons of bravery,
Two cups of creativity with a handful of honesty.

Mix all ingredients together with a big heart,
Bake for eleven years,
Once all baked, add two blue eyes,
Some blonde hair and throw lots of freckles on top of it.
This will make me.
Honest, kind, caring and creative.

Amelia Marsh (11)

Greenbank Preparatory School, Cheadle Hulme

This Is Me

My name is Charlotte and I'm ten years old,
My mum said when they made me they broke the mould!
I love playing with slime and trying on make-up and dresses,
My dad is always nagging me to clean up my messes.
To be kind and caring I try my very best.

Although my big brother calls me a pest!
Horse riding is the sport I love most,
My dream is to ride with the wind in my hair along the coast,
I spend most of my free time with my pets,
So it's not surprising my dream job is at the vets!

Charlotte Dicks (10)
Greenbank Preparatory School, Cheadle Hulme

This Is Me

I think I'm smart,
But my mum says I've got a permanent brain fart.
I think I'm cool,
My mum says, "Don't be a fool!"
When I go home I hear,
"Have you got any homework?"
That's my cue to groan,
I love gaming you see,
And trust me,
I think it is good for me!
I love rugby and for once,
My mum does agree,
But she also says I'm lazy,
I say, "You're crazy!"
She says I'm silly,
And actually,
I agree.

Seth Hughes (11)
Greenbank Preparatory School, Cheadle Hulme

This Is Me

This is me,
My name is Gigi,
And it's time for me to show you,
What my favourite pastime will be.

I throw it and catch it,
I dodge and blast,
I have to run really rather fast,
Scoring goals is the aim of the game,
This sport only lasts four quarters,
Which I think is quite a shame.

Have you guessed this sport yet?
Yes! It's netball.
This is my favourite thing to do,
Why don't you give it a try too?

Gigi Switzer (10)
Greenbank Preparatory School, Cheadle Hulme

Me!

You need:
A brain that likes conundrums and crosswords,
A bookworm,
A bit of kindness,
Some fun,
A good football defender.
How to make:
First, take a bookworm,
Add a bit of kindness,
Make another mixture of fun and the brain that likes conundrums and crosswords,
Pour it all into one big mixture,
Add a sprinkle of good football defender,
Bake for eleven years,
Add black hair and brown eyes,
You made me!

Yousaf Rafiq (11)
Greenbank Preparatory School, Cheadle Hulme

This Is Me

I would like to tell you about me,
And all the things I want to be.
My inspirations are Rosa and Anne,
I'm trying to be like them the best I can.
Rosa is fierce like a lion and fought to get people on her side,
While Anne was brave but had to hide.
But I think it's safe to say that Rosa and Anne were heroes of their day.
I hope that I will be as brave as they've been,
So that hopefully my strength will one day be seen.

Madeleine Lewis (10)
Greenbank Preparatory School, Cheadle Hulme

This Is Me!

I am curious, kind and caring,

A n awesome aeroplane pilot one day I will be,
M arvellous, merry and helpful,

G entle and pleasingly polite.
E nergetic and terrific at tennis,
O ne day I will fantastically fly,
R eliable and respectful, guitar I like to play,
G reat, funny friend I will always be,
E asy-going every day, I am glad to be me.

George Woolley (10)
Greenbank Preparatory School, Cheadle Hulme

My Family

The things I love is my family, sports and animals,
And much more.
I watch out on the world around me,
To see if there's anything to do.

But most of the time everyone is being in their own environment.

Me and my family sometimes do movie nights,
If not that, we can play a game,
But they still encourage me not to forget,
My studies and spending time outside to help me with my health.

Neal Vora (10)
Greenbank Preparatory School, Cheadle Hulme

This Is Me

I like to have lots of fun,
Normally in the sun,
I like lots of lovely sports,
Cricket and football I was taught.

I love my family, my sisters, mum and dad,
Nothing ever happens that is bad,
Everyone is as good as gold,
I can be quite silly,
But I'm also skinny.

I like science and maths,
Especially all the crafts,
But my dream is to be a scientist.

Ibrahim Ghafoor (10)
Greenbank Preparatory School, Cheadle Hulme

My Favourite Animal

My favourite animal is quite small,
But has big amounts of energy,
He has a moist black nose and excitement like confetti.
I can hear his paws patting from a planet away,
Usually when he wants to come and play.
His fluffy ears and adorable glare,
Lightens up my day.
I see him now,
I adore him so much,
With his waggy tail and his exciting punch.

Zak Martin (10)
Greenbank Preparatory School, Cheadle Hulme

This Is Me!

My name is Dove and I'm going to tell you what I love,
I like my hair but when I do it it hurts everywhere.
I'm bright, fair and fun, I'm always aiming to be number one.
One of my goals is to become an actress,
I really want to become famous.
This is me and I'm exactly who I want to be!

Dove Nguem (11)
Greenbank Preparatory School, Cheadle Hulme

This Is Me!

I am me.
No one else,
Just me.
And I am proud that I am,
I am strong,
I am weak,
I am brave,
I am scared,
I am happy,
I am sad,
And most of all,
I am not perfect.
I am not everything you and I want me to be,
But I am me,
And that's quite alright.

Harriet Heinekey (10)
Greenbank Preparatory School, Cheadle Hulme

Antarctica

When I am older,
I would like to explore Antarctica.
It might be a bit colder,
But I am sure it will be amazing!
Everything will be white,
It's very far to ride on a bike!
I will see lots of amazing animals,
Like polar bears, penguins and much more.
It will be as snowy as Christmas,
This will be the greatest trip I'm sure!

Poppy Pinkstone (10)
Gunter Primary School, Pype Hayes

What Makes Me Happy

When I'm sad I feel mad,
When I'm mad I feel sad,
But what makes me happy is spending time with my dad,
But when I see his face he puts a smile straight on my face,
If I'm not with my dad I like spending time with the rest of my family,
I like playing on my Xbox like a baby likes sucking its dummy,
And I like putting food in my tummy.

Alexandra Edwards (10)
Gunter Primary School, Pype Hayes

This Is Me

This is me!
I am nobody else,
I wouldn't change me for the world,
There's no doubt.
I can be happy, I can be sad,
I can be good, I can be bad!
But this is me!
I'm as free as a bird, as loud as a word,
I can be noisy and go *bang!*
I can be quiet and go *whisper!*
But I am me, I am me!
I'm not anybody else.

Isabell Swinburn (9)
Gunter Primary School, Pype Hayes

This Is Me

O v, is my nickname, my family likes calling me Ov!
V ery fast, I'm fast!
A thletic is me, I like sport!
N oisy is me, I like being loud!
D rink, my favourite drink is Fanta!
E ating is me, I love eating, my favourite food is a burger!
R eading is cool, I love reading books!

Ovander Delaney (9)
Gunter Primary School, Pype Hayes

Me, Micah

M icah, the fighter on fire like a lighter,
I 'm funny like bunnies, I'm fast and make a bash,
C helsea I cheer, also fear, don't want them to lose.
A ll I eat are apples and pears,
H ate when I fear, creepy nightmares, find a fiend of darkness and run straight out of there!

Micah Robinson (9)
Gunter Primary School, Pype Hayes

When I Am Older

When I am older I would own a dog,
A great companion by your side,
When you are sad you'll have a good time,
When you are grumpy they'll bark in your ear,
When you take it for a walk and it is fed,
Once you've seen it, the mud you dread,
As you can tell, I think dogs are the best!

Emily Fellows (10)
Gunter Primary School, Pype Hayes

All About Me

H ermiela is my name,
E xtreme runner is my goal,
R eally amazing reader,
M cDonald's lover, burger muncher,
I like football, scoring a goal,
E lephant, my favourite creature,
L over of dancing,
A mazing singer.

Hermiela Mogos (9)
Gunter Primary School, Pype Hayes

Oreo The Cat

He's fluffy and puffy,
He's cute and he would lick you.
He likes to run and have fun.
He likes Harry Potter,
And likes to holler,
Plays football,
He is lean and mean.
He eats and screams.
Sleeps and cleans.
He goes on a mat and catches a rat.

Ayaan Fazil (9)
Gunter Primary School, Pype Hayes

What I Like

Hi, my name is Fid,
I am nice, as smooth as ice!
The food I eat is good just like noodles!
I am happy but very jumpy!
The last thing I like is making videos,
Also, I like to sing a lot in my head!
I like playing football but sometimes I fall.

Fidyan Masum (9)
Gunter Primary School, Pype Hayes

All About Me!

H eat burns my skin,
A lways try my hardest,
R esilient!
R ain stings my skin,
I ntelligent!
S pace is a great topic,
O range is my favourite,
N ature is key!

Harrison Bird (10)
Gunter Primary School, Pype Hayes

Football

I like playing football, it makes me relax,
I like playing in defence because I'm good at it,
I like playing with my friends,
I like playing in the sun,
I like playing with my family.

Dewon Montaque (9)
Gunter Primary School, Pype Hayes

This Is Me

One thing about me is I can box,
And if you fight me you will get dropped,
Let's not talk about that,
We can be friends,
We can play games,
We can have fun.

Deacon Kelly (10)
Gunter Primary School, Pype Hayes

Everything About Me

M arcus talks a lot,
A ll he wants to be is an electrician,
R eally fast,
C ool!
U sually happy,
S ometimes sad.

Marcus Bryant (10)
Gunter Primary School, Pype Hayes

Gamer God

I am a gamer!
I don't like strangers!
Vegetables are the worst,
They make my mouth burst!
I have an Xbox,
And I hate the story 'Goldilocks'.

Alfie Conroy (9)
Gunter Primary School, Pype Hayes

All About Me!

A roller coaster of emotions!
Loud and noisy,
My favourite colour is red,
And I love berries!
And I am always very merry!

Addison Moore (9)
Gunter Primary School, Pype Hayes

My Different Worlds

The first thing I think of is scoring the winning goal,
In front of the cheering crowd hoping to make them proud,
The ref blows for a foul, all my teammates howl,
I score a hat-trick, I get the ball, all my teammates stand up tall.

My next world is a trip in my shining rocket ship,
People see the shooting stars, just missing Planet Mars,
The spaceman walks on the moon, I hope to see him soon,
The moon tonight is a crescent and the stars are bright and fluorescent.

My last world is, a very loving mummy and she's very sunny,
My Andrew is non-lyrical, if he gets a song right it's a miracle,
I have a crazy brother who loves to discover,
My dog Bronte is black and he knows how to track,
These are my different worlds.

Isaac O'Brien (9)
Hatfield Woodhouse Primary School, Hatfield Woodhouse

Grayson, Gray Gray, Go Go, G

Grayson, Gray Gray, Go Go, G,
Are just some of the names that are used for me!

I'm a bookworm of a boy with an inquisitive mind,
I'm thoughtful, sensitive, one of a kind!

I love online gaming with all of my friends,
But I hate it at bedtime when game time ends.

As I sleep in my bed I look forward to dawn,
Because that is the time when gamers respawn.

At the age of nine, I'm still very young,
So it's impossible to say what is yet to come.

I'll keep working hard and doing my best,
And mum and dad will take care of the rest!

Grayson Golightly (9)
Hatfield Woodhouse Primary School, Hatfield Woodhouse

My Magnificent Mum

My magnificent mum, long ago,
Taught me everything I know.
To talk, to walk and everything I do,
And every step, she's been there too.

My magnificent mum.

She was there when I said my first word,
She is the leader of my herd.
She hugs me when I'm feeling down,
And turns my frown upside down.

My magnificent mum is there every day,
And is practically perfect in every way.
My magnificent mum means the world to me,
And that's how it will always be for eternity.

Lilly-Mai Ramsey (10)
Hatfield Woodhouse Primary School, Hatfield Woodhouse

Pony Art

I am Sophia, as wise as can be,
There is nobody as happy and smiley as me,
I love horses and they love me,
My favourite little pony is called TC,
When I'm trotting up and down I never wear a frown,
He makes me so proud he deserves a crown,
But my biggest love of all is my art,
Of which I draw from my heart,
Of all things I love the most,
Are Mum, Dad and Erin who I keep very close,
So this is my poem, this is me,
I hope it makes you as happy as can be.

Sophia Wilcock (7)
Hatfield Woodhouse Primary School, Hatfield Woodhouse

Edward The Entertainer

There is a lad who likes to dance,
His favourite move is a hop and a prance.
He likes to learn, his favourite subject is maths,
And instead of showers he loves to take baths.
When Edward feels down in the dumps you send a friend round the bend,
To help Edward back into his trend.
He rides his bike down the lane,
His family loves that he's fun and insane.
When he grows up he wants to shine brighter than any star and drive a fast car.

Edward Camplejohn (8)
Hatfield Woodhouse Primary School, Hatfield Woodhouse

My Animal Kingdom

I close my eyes,
A gateway appears to my animal world,
The trees are green,
The sun is bright,
The animals come at my very sight.

I see the geckos lying on rocks,
I hear kookaburras laughing,
The camels drinking from the basin,
Leopards hiding in the grass.

It makes me happy to see nature,
And watch the magic unfold,
I can be in the rainforest or the wilderness,
All I have to do is close my eyes.

Edward O'Brien (9)
Hatfield Woodhouse Primary School, Hatfield Woodhouse

My Life

I'm a superstar footballer rocking the goal,
I'm the king of all chillers sleeping alone,
I'm the most silly one of the group being crazy all day,
I'm very adventurous exploring the world,
I'm pretty smart walking down the hall,
I'm very friendly being a good friend,
I'm very excited jumping all around,
I'm very fun playing all the games,
I'm very kind, helping people out.

Ellis Finney (8)
Hatfield Woodhouse Primary School, Hatfield Woodhouse

Fancy Nancy

I'm kind and friendly,
Smart and funny,
Passionate about the things I love,
And always seem to forget one glove,
I hate eating peas,
And walks that involve bees,
My favourite hobby is dancing,
Mum says I'm always prancing,
To which I always disagree,
I may be a bit silly,
But I'm not a dally-dilly!
My name is Nancy,
This is me!

Nancy Wigglesworth (7)
Hatfield Woodhouse Primary School, Hatfield Woodhouse

Nature

Nature is my favourite thing because it makes me happy and calm.
In summer the grass is lush and green.
In autumn the leaves are coloured just like a fire red, yellow and orange.
In winter nature has to survive through the wild winds and stormy rain.
In spring the flowers pop out with vibrant colours.
Every season brings different things to see, hear and smell.

Orla Torn (9)
Hatfield Woodhouse Primary School, Hatfield Woodhouse

The Little Artist

G reat at art like a painter,
E xcellent at drawing like an artist,
O riginally good at designing like a designer,
R eally good at creativity like a crafty person,
G orgeously good at painting like a watercolourist,
I ncredibly good at sketching like an illustrator,
A mazing at making stuff like a crafter.

Georgia Hornsby (10)
Hatfield Woodhouse Primary School, Hatfield Woodhouse

Ronaldo

Ronaldo can shoot from ten yards in,
And he'll hit it top bin.
Round the defence and through midfield,
He'll run,
Just like a shooting gun.
Tackling Messi and megsing Son,
Passes down the wing he'll get on.
In front of the keeper, he can't miss,
Come on Ronaldo you've got this.

Harry Houghton (9)
Hatfield Woodhouse Primary School, Hatfield Woodhouse

Who Am I?

T hey call me Emma,
H ow are you?
I am friendly, kind and curious,
S illy sometimes too!

I like to paint and draw a lot,
S ometimes a volcano that's very hot.

M y favourite colour is blue,
E nough is said! What about you?

Emma Mikolkova (7)
Hatfield Woodhouse Primary School, Hatfield Woodhouse

This Is Me

T his poem is about me,
H appy as can be,
I am friendly and kind,
S porty and fine.

I love my family and friends,
S illy is what I love to do.

M aking crafts is very fun,
E xciting when they are done.

Sophie Kirk (7)
Hatfield Woodhouse Primary School, Hatfield Woodhouse

Me, Myself And I

T alkative as a magpie,
H appy as a lark,
I s as bright as a button,
S weet as sugar.

I s as friendly as a puppy,
S mart as a whip.

M ischievous as a kitten,
E legant as a feather.

Heidi Foster (8)
Hatfield Woodhouse Primary School, Hatfield Woodhouse

Cr7

He wears number seven,
He started at Lisbon,
Scoring goals,
Like no tomorrow,
It's Ronaldo.

He's jumped two metres,
That's not human,
He's won the Champions League,
Too many times,
It's Ronaldo.

Benjamin Hatton (10)
Hatfield Woodhouse Primary School, Hatfield Woodhouse

My Favourite Animal

A creature of land and sea,
It lives on ice,
It is white,
Eats fish,
Its fur keeps it warm,
Swim days at a time,
Smells its prey from ages away,
Largest living creature on land,
What is it?

Answer: A polar bear.

Amelia Dawes (8)
Hatfield Woodhouse Primary School, Hatfield Woodhouse

My Favourite Game

It's a building game,
It's a level game,
It's very complicated,
It's a boss game,
It's a platformer game,
It's a live game,
It's a Nintendo game.
What is it?

Answer: Super Mario Maker 2.

Jadon Davies (7)
Hatfield Woodhouse Primary School, Hatfield Woodhouse

Dog Lover

I love the way you smile,
I love your gentle kiss,
I love the way you cheer me up when you play hide-and-seek,
I love my fluffy friend,
I love your loyal gentle soul,
I love your big puppy eyes,
And your gorgeous face.

Miriam Daisy Cottingham Taylorson (8)
Hatfield Woodhouse Primary School, Hatfield Woodhouse

A Man With Skill

A man who was a,
Teacher for drama,
He made me laugh he,
Gets no karma,
Idea for a book denied at first,
That was the birth of Horrible Histories,
The man was,
Terry Deary.

Isabella Watson (10)
Hatfield Woodhouse Primary School, Hatfield Woodhouse

Oliver's Chocolate Brownie Poem

Mix the butter and the sugar,
Make it nice and smooth,
Add the cocoa and the chocolate,
Then dance around the room,
I love to bake brownies because,
They're yummy like my mummy!

Oliver Stewart (7)
Hatfield Woodhouse Primary School, Hatfield Woodhouse

Football

F un,
O utside,
O n the pitch,
T ackling,
B ack of the net,
A ll celebrate,
L ots of fun,
L eft wing is where I play!

Jacob Jackson (7)
Hatfield Woodhouse Primary School, Hatfield Woodhouse

Rabbit

R is for rosy cheeks,
A is for love of animals,
B is for beautiful,
B is for blue eyes,
I is for imaginary,
T is for thoughtful.

Caitlin Beasley (10)
Hatfield Woodhouse Primary School, Hatfield Woodhouse

This Is Noah

N obody in the world quite like me,
O ne in a million,
A mazing it is to be me,
H appy am I to be the only Noah I can be.

Noah Massingham (10)
Hatfield Woodhouse Primary School, Hatfield Woodhouse

Silly Billy

I have a dog called Billy,
Sometimes he's very silly,
He jumps and leaps,
And barks in his sleep,
That's why he's Silly Billy!

Dale Hibbitt (7)
Hatfield Woodhouse Primary School, Hatfield Woodhouse

Faye Rocks

F aye is me,
A Geologist is what I would like to be,
Y es, I like rocks,
E arthquakes and volcanic blocks.

Faye Severn (10)
Hatfield Woodhouse Primary School, Hatfield Woodhouse

This Is All About Me

I am fun,
I am sporty,
I am happy,
I am kind,
I am adventurous,
I am friendly,
This is all about me!

Esme Massingham (8)
Hatfield Woodhouse Primary School, Hatfield Woodhouse

I Love...

I love all animals,
Especially a dog called Arlo.
I love to play games,
I beat my family at Uno!
I love swimming,
Lessons can be a bit scary.
I love my Nintendo Switch,
My favourite game is Animal Crossing.
I love going to Stagecoach,
We do singing, dancing and acting.
I love riding my bike,
Now I can ride on two wheels.
I love sweeties,
I try and sneak lots into my bedroom.
I love drawing pictures for my mummy,
They always make her smile.
I love cooking with my nan,
We made pizza and I put it in the oven.
I love reading David Walliams books,
They make me laugh.

I love my family,
Because they love me!

Orla Caldwell-Giles (7)
Langmoor Primary School, Oadby

About Me

My name is Lillie and I like painting and drawing,
My favourite animal is a bunny and the colours I like are violet and galaxy colours,
My best friends are Charlotte and Fraya and Erin,
My favourite fruit is cherries and lemon,
I like watching football with my brother and my favourite game is Twister.

Lillie Green (7)
Langmoor Primary School, Oadby

I Am Charlotte

I am Charlotte and I am kind and helpful.
I work hard and do my best so you shall too.
I can keep calm and do my best so you should do as well.
I help others and it can be you so please do help too.
I am grateful and you can be too,
But you have to say thank you.

Charlotte Watts (7)
Langmoor Primary School, Oadby

Happiness

Happiness is fun because,
I can play in the sun.

Spending long days in the pool,
Helps keep me cool.

The garden is where I play,
Each and every single day.

I enjoy learning to bake,
Yummy, scrumptious cupcakes.

Erin Knight
Langmoor Primary School, Oadby

All About Me!

C onquering my fear of,
H eights and bridges,
A voids doing sport except dodgeball,
R eally like to do stories,
L iving in Borneo as,
I love orangutans,
E njoying Pompa's soup

Charlie Picton (7)
Langmoor Primary School, Oadby

What Makes Me Tiago

T echnology is interesting,
I am kind, intelligent and helpful,
A pes are my favourite animal,
G aming is my favourite hobby,
O utstanding is what I like to be.

Tiago Sood (8)
Langmoor Primary School, Oadby

This Is Me

T ed is my name and I like baking with
E veryone, as we all take turns to stir, I
D on't like poems, I'll just stop now.

S o that is the end.

Ted Smith (8)
Langmoor Primary School, Oadby

This Is Me

S ahib likes basketball,
A lways happy to help,
H e likes maths,
I like playing with my friends,
B e a person that can share and care.

Sahib Shergill (8)
Langmoor Primary School, Oadby

Fraya Poem

My name is Fraya,
My age is eight,
My house has a big blue gate,
I live with my brother, my dad and my mum,
At the weekend we like to have fun.

Fraya Turner (8)
Langmoor Primary School, Oadby

This Is Me

Kamryn is a nine-year-old, average-sized,
Scottish girl,
With long, wavy, blonde hair,
And sky blue eyes,
She lives in Strathy Point,
In the far north of Scotland,
Kamryn is a funny, playful person,
But can be a bit loud at times!
She loves to draw and play with her friends,
Her favourite day of the week is Friday,
Because it is half a day at school,
Kamryn dislikes clowns and huge spiders,
As she finds both terrifying!
Her ambition is to become a pet sitter,
She is so happy when her friends come over to play,
Or when she goes to a friends house,
Her best friends are Emily Farquhar,
Emily Mackay and Eevie Mackay,
Who is her cousin,
Kamryn loves her family.

Kamryn Mackay (9)
Melvich Primary School, Melvich

This Is Me

Merryn is a small, slim girl,
With long blonde hair and grey-blue eyes,
She lives in Melvich with her mum, dad,
And two sisters,
Merryn is always cheerful,
And her family says she talks loudly,
She likes going to her cousin Ava's farm,
Merryn dislikes spiders,
Her favourite day of the week is Friday,
Because her dad takes her and her sister,
Megan, to the Coastline Coffee Shop,
Just up the road from where she lives,
She is delighted when summer comes,
Because she gets to see her cousins,
Jackson and Gemma,
And it's her birthday too,
Her ambition is to be a zookeeper,
Or a teacher,
Merryn is happy to be in a loving family.

Merryn Murray (10)
Melvich Primary School, Melvich

This Is Me

Megan is a tall, slim, eight-year-old girl,
With long, auburn hair and blue eyes.
She lives in a small village called Melvich,
In the far north of Scotland.
Megan is a kind, helpful person,
But her sisters say she can be annoying at times.
She loves to do gymnastics, horse riding,
And swimming.
Her favourite day of the week is Saturday,
Because she goes to gymnastics.
Megan dislikes snakes.
Her ambition is either to be a gymnastics coach,
Or work on a farm.
She is delighted when summer comes,
And December because it is her birthday,
And Christmas.
Megan loves her family.

Megan Murray (9)
Melvich Primary School, Melvich

This Is Me

Benjamin is a tall, nine-year-old boy,
With short blonde hair and blue eyes,
He lives in Melvich,
In the far north of Scotland,
Benjamin is a kind, happy person,
But can get bored easily,
He likes to play with his Hot Wheels,
And play football with his friends,
His favourite day is Saturday,
Because he gets to play with his Hot Wheels,
Benjamin dislikes wasps,
Because he thinks they might sting him,
His ambition is to become an actor,
He is delighted when September comes,
Because it is his birthday on the fourteenth,
Benjamin is happy to be alive.

Benjamin Mackinnon (10)
Melvich Primary School, Melvich

This Is Me

Stanley is a tall eight-year-old boy,
With blonde hair and blue eyes,
He lives in the small village of Melvich,
In the north of Scotland,
Stanley is a kind, hard-working person,
But he can be a bit noisy sometimes,
He loves to have play fights with his dog,
Sasha.
His favourite day of the week is Friday,
Because he leaves school early,
Stanley dislikes spiders,
Because some of them are venomous and can kill you,
His ambition is to be a vet,
He loves Christmas and Easter and his birthday,
Which is in August,
Stanley is very happy to be alive.

Stanley Bird (8)
Melvich Primary School, Melvich

This Is Me

Calum is a small, fast, ten-year-old boy,
With short brown hair and brown eyes,
He lives in Strathy,
In the far north of Scotland,
He is a friendly, healthy person,
But can be a little bad-tempered sometimes,
Calum loves playing football with his friends,
His favourite day is Friday,
Because he gets to see his friends and relax,
He dislikes littering,
Because it harms the planet,
Calum's ambition,
Is to become a professional football player,
He is delighted when March comes,
Because it is his birthday,
Calum is happy to be alive.

Calum Farquhar (10)
Melvich Primary School, Melvich

This Is Me

Emily is an average height, slim girl,
With shoulder-length, dark hair,
And dark brown eyes,
She lives in Strathy in the far north of,
Scotland,
Emily is a bubbly, cheerful person,
But can be impatient at times,
She loves to play Roblox,
And go swimming,
Her favourite day of the week is Friday,
Because it is the start of the weekend,
Emily dislikes cats,
And finds them quite scary,
Her ambition is to become a vet,
She is delighted when November comes,
And her birthday approaches,
Emily loves her family.

Emily Farquhar (9)
Melvich Primary School, Melvich

This Is Me

Aurelia is a tall, slim girl,
With shoulder-length, dark brown hair,
Hazel eyes and tanned skin.
She lives in Strathalladale,
In the far north of Scotland.
Aurelia is a caring person,
And gets excited when she sees her family.
She loves chilling out,
And chatting while listening to music.
Her favourite day is Friday,
Because school ends early,
Her grandpa comes to visit,
And she has lots of fun with him.
Aurelia dislikes swearing.
Her ambition is to be better in life.
Aurelia loves her family.

Aurelia Sweeting (8)
Melvich Primary School, Melvich

This Is Me

Mati is a small, slim, eight-year-old boy,
With blonde hair and blue eyes,
He lives in Melvich in the north of Scotland,
Mati is a happy boy,
But sometimes he forgets his manners,
He loves to play football and build things outside,
His favourite day of the week is Friday,
Because school finishes early that day,
Mati dislikes spiders and mice,
His ambition is to be a scientist,
He is delighted when it is Christmas,
And his birthday because he gets lots of presents,
Mati is glad to be alive.

Mati Ilski (9)
Melvich Primary School, Melvich

This Is Me

Connor is a fast, tall eight-year-old boy,
With short brown hair and blue eyes,
He lives in Craggy with his mum,
And little brother called Logan,
He loves animals and his BMX bike,
His favourite day is Thursday,
Because it is PE,
Connor dislikes heights,
His ambition is to be a rapper,
He is delighted when it is April,
Because it is his birthday,
Connor is glad to be alive.

Connor Crossley (8)
Melvich Primary School, Melvich

This Is Me!

T hinks that Pokémon are the best
H as Pokémon brilliant and shining pearl
I 've got four Gym badges on Pokémon brilliant diamond
S o I'm trying to get the badge in Heart Hoe gym

I love Metagross and Zygard
S ometimes I have a Pokémon battle with Mrs Willims and Mrs Yates

M yself and Kade both love Pokémon
E very time I go to Grandad's house I have fun with Grandad and Nana, it makes us laugh.

Jack Hatfield (9)
Ryhill Junior, Infant & Nursery School, Ryhill

This Is Me

T iny with blonde, bright vanilla hair
H as one brother and stepsisters
I like sleeping and being lazy and my family and animals
S chool is my favourite place to visit and do learning

I love my family and friends
S ometimes I have a movie night with them

M y favourite ice cream flavour is chocolate
E specially with strawberry toppings.

Molly Carr (9)
Ryhill Junior, Infant & Nursery School, Ryhill

This Is Me

My eyes are blue like the Atlantic Ocean,
My hair is as brown as a monkey,
I'm a gamer not a hater,
My cheeks are as red as an apple,
I'm tiny but I'm very whiny and shiny,
I like bananas but I'm not a 'nana,
I have a bike but don't ride,
I'm nice as pie,
When you see me fly,
You know I like these rhymes,
I'm crazy but I'm shady.

Kate Mclauchlan (9)
Ryhill Junior, Infant & Nursery School, Ryhill

Be Yourself

T all with warm red hair
H as one dog that is fluffy and white
I like playing outside with my dog
S ome things I like are space to see the weird planets

I love my dog and my mum and dad
S ometimes I go on walks with them in the rain and get wet

M y favourite rapper is XXXTentacion
E leven is my favourite number.

Freddie Nunn (9)
Ryhill Junior, Infant & Nursery School, Ryhill

This Is Me!

Hello, my name is Miller,
I'll put you through a thriller.

I play a lot of football,
It's my favourite sport out of them all.

My favourite subject is PE,
It will really help me.

My favourite animal is a dog,
My least favourite weather is fog.

Now you can see all about me,
Which will show,
This is me!

Miller Lee Bramley (9)
Ryhill Junior, Infant & Nursery School, Ryhill

This Is Me!

T all with long brown hair
H as two brothers and a dog
I love my family
S onny is my brother's name

I love my grandad, mum and dad and grandma
S ometimes I go shopping with my grandma and grandad

M y mum always takes me to the play area
E very holiday I like to swim in a pool.

Scarlett Cadman (8)
Ryhill Junior, Infant & Nursery School, Ryhill

This Will Always Be Me

When I am up,
I will always get a cup.
It will always have tea,
And that is what you need to know about me.
I'll be playing football,
But when I find out it's raining I'd bawl.
While it's raining,
Inside I will be gaming.
When I'm doing maths,
All I'll be thinking about is a bath.
This will always be me.

James Mallinder (9)
Ryhill Junior, Infant & Nursery School, Ryhill

This Is About Me

T all with hard hair
H as an annoying brother
I love lying on my comfortable bed
S pain is my favourite place to go

I love playing football
S ometimes I go on a ride with my family

M e and my family like eating Sunday dinner
E lephants are my favourite animal.

Callan Church (9)
Ryhill Junior, Infant & Nursery School, Ryhill

All About Me

T all with warm red hair
H as two nice brothers
I love spending time with my family
S omething I like is being at home

I love horse riding on my favourite horse
S ometimes I go on lovely walks with my family

M y favourite animals are dogs and horses
E specially like the movies.

Isla Henderson (8)
Ryhill Junior, Infant & Nursery School, Ryhill

This Will Always Be Me!

When I am sad I am a rain cloud,
But when I am happy I am up and loud.
I am the youngest,
And I am the funniest.
My sister likes to bake,
Not I, but I will eat the cake.
My mum is good at making tea,
It's nice to eat but cooking is not for me.
My dad enjoys cutting the lawn,
But when I see him I start to yawn.

Tia Earl (10)
Ryhill Junior, Infant & Nursery School, Ryhill

Be You

T all with light soft hair
H as three siblings and two cats
I love my hairy two cats
S omething I love is space to find new planets

I love XXXTentacion because he is cool
S omething else I like is maths

M y favourite game is FIFA
E very holiday I go to Spain.

Max Miller (9)
Ryhill Junior, Infant & Nursery School, Ryhill

This Is About Me!

T all with long hair
H as two sisters
I love everyone in my family
S omething I love is going on holiday

I love going to Ibiza with family
S ometimes I draw on my own

M e and my family like to walk my dog
E very Sunday me and my family have Sunday dinner.

Lilly-May Lawton (8)
Ryhill Junior, Infant & Nursery School, Ryhill

This Will Always Be Me!

T iny or tall I'll play football,
H onesty is my power,
I am a little crazy,
S ometimes I get angry.

I really love my family,
S piders are my biggest fear.

M y name is Evie,
E xcellent as a goalkeeper.

Now you can see,
This is me!

Evie Broadhead (9)
Ryhill Junior, Infant & Nursery School, Ryhill

This Is Me

T all with shiny blonde hair
H as a dog who is brown and fluffy
I love spending time with my family
S ummer holidays are the best

I love my family very much
S ometimes I go on walks with them

M e and my brother like playing
E specially I love my pets.

Jesse Bryan (8)
Ryhill Junior, Infant & Nursery School, Ryhill

I Love My Dogs

I'm a dog lover.
My dog is vicious and she sleeps like a bat,
But no matter what,
I will always love her to the moon and back.
She is a biter but it is to protect,
She is a gem.
My other dog is as daft as a bat,
She is playful and fluffy.
My dogs are called Millie and Pipie,
They are funny.

Evie Mai Jowitt (9)
Ryhill Junior, Infant & Nursery School, Ryhill

This Is My Life

T all with curly brown hair
H as a big-eyed goldfish
I love fishing with my dad
S ummer is the best month

I like rugby and Pokémon
S ometimes I go out for dinner

M y favourite game is Animal Crossing
E very day is good.

Freddy Atmore (9)
Ryhill Junior, Infant & Nursery School, Ryhill

This Is Me

T all with browny blond hair
H as an incredible mum
I like playing Fortnite
S ometimes I'm mean

I love my mum and dad
S ometimes I watch movies with them

M y favourite food is steak
E specially with peppercorn sauce.

Otis Ferron (8)
Ryhill Junior, Infant & Nursery School, Ryhill

This Is Me

A kennings poem

I am a...
Dog lover,
Cat hater,
Lego builder,
Early waker,
Older brother,
Cake eater,
Game player,
Music lover,
Sister helper,
Family lover,
Hard worker,
Phone owner,
YouTube watcher,
Money spender,
Puppy cuddler.

This is me!

Joshua Johnson (11)
Ryhill Junior, Infant & Nursery School, Ryhill

This Is My Hobby

This is one of my hobbies, it's very fun,
I had lots of practice and now I am good,
I am very exhausted when I am done,
It's my favourite sport, you have to be fit,
I have to practise every week,
I watch it on TV, it's entertaining,
So now you know what my hobby is.

Ben Ellis (9)
Ryhill Junior, Infant & Nursery School, Ryhill

I Have Different Football Skills

I can shoot like Cristiano Ronaldo,
The pace of Lionel Messi,
The passing skills of Virgil van Dijk,
The physical ability of Neymar,
The defending of Ibrahima Konate,
The dribbling like Mohamad Salah,
The celebrations like Mason Mount.

This is me!

Lucas Sagar (10)
Ryhill Junior, Infant & Nursery School, Ryhill

Grizzy, The Lemmings And Me

I love the Lemmings and Grizzy,
And they all love me.
We all like yummy spread!
Mrs Land is the best,
She teaches us in school,
She is kind and sharing and cool.
We all (except Grizzy) watch the loud house,
Mice will hide from our beautiful house.

Kade Parkinson (9)
Ryhill Junior, Infant & Nursery School, Ryhill

This Is Me

T all with red hair
H as a cat called Murphy
I love pasta carbonara
S ometimes I talk too much

I love my mum
S ometimes I play

M aybe I will be a teacher
E very day I have fun.

Flynn McCabe (8)
Ryhill Junior, Infant & Nursery School, Ryhill

This Is Me

My name is Lana I'm so cool,
But I'm really not a fool,
I'm really tall,
My friend is small,
Her name is Lily,
She is not silly,
My eyes are brown,
And I don't like to frown,
My dog is Max,
He can tell some facts.

Lana Cabas (9)
Ryhill Junior, Infant & Nursery School, Ryhill

This Is Me

I like gaming and I play football.
My name starts with M and ends with N.
And I love running.
I have a cousin, she is very nice.
She is my favourite.
Who am I?
P.S. You are special in your own way.

Answer: Myself, Mason.

Mason Watson (9)
Ryhill Junior, Infant & Nursery School, Ryhill

Eleanor H's Poem

I am as brave as a fox,
I have a brain as big as a box.
I can be as sad as a rain cloud,
But sometimes I can read a bit loud.
I can be fast,
I can be strong,
But it won't be long,
Till I come up with a song.

Eleanor Hope (10)
Ryhill Junior, Infant & Nursery School, Ryhill

I Love Art

I love art,
It gives me a spark!
When I am painting,
It keeps me concentrating.
My favourite colour is pink,
But I don't mind using other ink.
And when I draw,
I enjoy myself more.

This is me!

Amy Corden (10)
Ryhill Junior, Infant & Nursery School, Ryhill

This Is Me

I am Lily,
And I'm not silly.
I am a star,
So hop in my car.
My friend is Lana,
She is not a banana.
I won't let her down, never,
Because we are best friends forever.

This is me!

Lily Alice Wicks (9)
Ryhill Junior, Infant & Nursery School, Ryhill

This Is Me

I am a happy person,

A nd I am a funny person,
M y family is very kind,

J ay is my name,
A lways playing my games,
Y oungest in the family.

Jay Fisher (9)
Ryhill Junior, Infant & Nursery School, Ryhill

Caiden A's Rap

I can run,
I can be fun.
I can laugh,
I can be daft,
I can survive on a raft.
I can shoot happy rays,
Which happens at my place.
As I game all night,
I party past daylight.

Caiden Armitage (11)
Ryhill Junior, Infant & Nursery School, Ryhill

This Is Me

My hair has the colour of a banana,
Everyone tells me I look like my nana.
My eyes are like blue marbles,
They are like the sky.
I am tiny but I'm shiny,
I am happy but not chatty.

Allana Margerrison (10)
Ryhill Junior, Infant & Nursery School, Ryhill

This Is Me

E xcellent helper,
B ee hater,
O riginal person,
N ice and kind,
E xtra caring,
Y oung and fun.

Eboney Smart (9)
Ryhill Junior, Infant & Nursery School, Ryhill

Just Me

G enerous and happy,
R eliable and kind,
A cceptable and quiet,
C heerful and smart,
E xcellent at art.

Grace Morris (9)
Ryhill Junior, Infant & Nursery School, Ryhill

The Brain Of A Spirited Girl

Untouched, uncharted by mankind,
Although it may be a little girl's mind.
A dash of mischief,
A hint of bliss,
A touch of veracity and an unexpected twist!
But what is this twist you ask?
In the end it shall be unmasked.
Mythical creatures, mammals that speak,
Are some of the wonders you can seek.
A tornado of thoughts, swirling with rage,
Can humans fly? Why do we age?
This dictionary-like brain, forages for words,
It scavenges and searches until something occurs.
In the back of this girl's brain,
All her revered memories remain.
Her first steps, her first hike,
The day she learned to ride a bike.
Before you leave, here's one last inkling:

This girl's imagination is still lingering... What is it? It's Abigail's brain!

Abigail Wielezew (9)
Wisbech St Mary CE (VA) Primary School, Wisbech St Mary

How To Make Me!

You will need:
A bucket of positivity,
One litre of giggles,
Two hundred millilitres of elegance,
One hundred percent of green eyes,
Fifty millilitres of a good sister,
Bowl of intelligence, an enormous bowl.

Method:
First, get the bowl of positivity into the bowl.
After that, pour one litre of giggles into the bowl.
Silently, listen to the stream of elegance going in.
Now, put one hundred per cent of the green eyes in.
Then, sprinkle fifty millilitres of a good sister in.
Finally, drizzle in the five hundred litres of intelligence and mix together.
Watch as a star rises, that star is me!

Georgie Cordery (10)
Wisbech St Mary CE (VA) Primary School, Wisbech St Mary

How To Make Me

What you need:
Two hundred litres of fun,
A pinch of mischief,
Dash of love for my puppy Daisy,
And sprinkles for dance, acro,
A cup full of love for people who aren't here.

What you do:
First, add two hundred litres of fun,
Next, add a pinch of mischief and mix them both together,
After that, add a cup of love for people who aren't here and mix that with a dash of love for my dog Daisy.
Finally, add sprinkles for dance and acro, mix them all together and you have made me.
Final note of warning, don't add fake friends as it will be ruined.

Riamae Boswell (9)
Wisbech St Mary CE (VA) Primary School, Wisbech St Mary

This Is Me

I'm Mercedes, I like cats and that's a fact.
I like sweets and also treats.
My favourite colour is baby-blue and I have a bunny called Clue.
In Year 5, it was World War One and it was pretty fun.
I live with a family of four, my house is never a bore.
I like all my friends especially Ella, she's my BFF, I know they will support me until the very end.
My house is never boring because I've got a crazy brother called Ebby and he's crazy and brazen.
I like koalas, they're my favourite, so cuddly like me.

Mercedes Neale
Wisbech St Mary CE (VA) Primary School, Wisbech St Mary

My Life

My name is Chase and this is my life...
When I was in school in Year 1,
I made friends, I had a ton.
In Year 2 I began to grow,
I learned about animals and things I didn't know!
Egypt was our topic in Year 3,
It was fascinating, we even made a mummy.
In Year 4 we studied the vicious Vikings,
They terrorised and stole to their likings.
In Year 5 was World War Two, the great war,
I was shocked and saddened by the horrors people saw.

Chase Finch (10)
Wisbech St Mary CE (VA) Primary School, Wisbech St Mary

This Is Me

I'm a super striker!
My rock-hard studs sink into the ground,
Like a knife through butter,
I tear through the grass with ease,
As I run fast on this cold winter's morning,
My feet are faster than a lightning bolt,
But now...
My chance is here,
I hit the ball with such power I think it popped,
In the blink of an eye it's passed the keeper,
And in the net, oh my god, that's outrageous.

Bobby Holmes (9)
Wisbech St Mary CE (VA) Primary School, Wisbech St Mary

Beautiful In Every Way

Roses are red, violets are blue,
I love myself,
And so should you,
You do not have to wear make-up today,
Because you are beautiful in every way,
You're beautiful when you're kind,
You're beautiful when you're happy,
You're beautiful when you're angry,
You're beautiful when you're sad,
But especially when you are just you!

Sophia Lee (9)
Wisbech St Mary CE (VA) Primary School, Wisbech St Mary

My Hero

Silky, hot cocoa hair,
Brave and fearless,
A funny attitude,
My hero every day,
Making me laugh,
Supporting me forever,
Kind as Snow White,
As funny as a chimp eating broccoli,
Animal keen,
Never mean,
Her heart is fine as a rose,
An exploding daydream of fun,
Have you guessed it yet?
Are you correct?
My, oh, my it's... Eve!

Hollie Payne (10)
Wisbech St Mary CE (VA) Primary School, Wisbech St Mary

All About Me

I'm as cuddly as a koala,
I'm as funny as can be,
I really love animals,
And that's a fact from me.
I want to become a horse rider,
And I'm scared of any sort of spider.
I'm lucky with my life at home,
My family and cats mean I'm never alone.
My friends are really kind to me,
When I'm down they make me happy.

Jazmin New (10)
Wisbech St Mary CE (VA) Primary School, Wisbech St Mary

A Boy Like Me

An imagination as high as the sky,
As free as a bird, I don't have to cry.
As tall as trees can go,
As funny as a monkey, I know.
Domino's is my favourite food,
I like to play basketball, I really do.
I love my hair, it shines in the sun,
And I really love to have fun.
In the morning I drink tea,
And this is me.

Jack Broker (10)
Wisbech St Mary CE (VA) Primary School, Wisbech St Mary

The Forest Florist

As if the tree was a florist,
Flower and fauna was strewn around.
She takes time to embed the flowers,
In the nutritious ground.
Spreading her love through the veins of petals and leaves,
The flower breathes!
As the love flows,
She knows.
That soon the bliss will bloom,
As if flowers were crawling up a love-filled room.

Tillie Bowett (10)
Wisbech St Mary CE (VA) Primary School, Wisbech St Mary

My Culture

I have long hair,
And I go to Appleby horse fair.

My favourite jewellery is golden,
I always respect my oldens.

I love being a part of my culture,
Surrounded by my family is ultra.

Dolly, a cob, pulls our horse and cart,
She has her very own special place in my heart.
This is my culture.

Lily Godwin (9)
Wisbech St Mary CE (VA) Primary School, Wisbech St Mary

Beach

Waves washing against the shore,
Being at home would be such a bore.
Sand squished between my toes,
Shells lined up on the beach in rows.
A seagull caws up ahead,
Heading home to rest its head.
The rockpools gleamed in the light,
I love the beach, what a sight!

Eve Clark (10)
Wisbech St Mary CE (VA) Primary School, Wisbech St Mary

Things I Like

I like art,
I like to draw planes,
But I hate it when it rains.
I like to play games too,
But I hate it when I lose,
I was eating my food,
But my mum told me to move,
I ran to my room watching YouTube in a mood.

Jake Gilson (9)
Wisbech St Mary CE (VA) Primary School, Wisbech St Mary

This Is Me

I love my friends,
Until the world ends.
My family,
Lives happily.
I enjoy games,
And I get my aims.
If I had an alien,
I'd call him Adrien.
I shall seek,
To be unique.

Ella Jayne Lemmon (9)
Wisbech St Mary CE (VA) Primary School, Wisbech St Mary

YOUNG WRITERS INFORMATION

We hope you have enjoyed reading this book – and that you will continue to in the coming years.

If you're the parent or family member of an enthusiastic poet or story writer, do visit our website www.youngwriters.co.uk/subscribe and sign up to receive news, competitions, writing challenges and tips, activities and much, much more! There's lots to keep budding writers motivated!

If you would like to order further copies of this book, or any of our other titles, then please give us a call or order via your online account.

Young Writers
Remus House
Coltsfoot Drive
Peterborough
PE2 9BF
(01733) 890066
info@youngwriters.co.uk

Join in the conversation!
Tips, news, giveaways and much more!

YoungWritersUK YoungWritersCW youngwriterscw